GETTING TO PERUGIA
Poems 1999-2002

By the same author:
THE SLEEPING PLACE
BEAUTIFUL COUNTRY

Iain Duggan

GETTING TO PERUGIA

Poems 1999-2002

THE ARIEL PRESS
MMII

GETTING TO PERUGIA
is published in November 2002 by
THE ARIEL PRESS
Francis Street, Wexford, Ireland

All rights Reserved
© Iain Duggan, 2002

This book is sold subject to the conditions that it shall not, by way of trade or otherwise, be lent, resold, hired out or otherwise circulated without the publisher's prior consent in any form or binding or cover other than that in which it is published and without a similar condition including this condition being imposed on the subsequent purchaser.

ISBN 0 9534369 2 6

Book & Cover Design: Lee Robinson
Front Cover Photograph: Goretti Rozairo
Back Cover Photograph: Oscar O'Leary

Typeset in Aldine 721 BT
and printed in the Republic of Ireland
at The Print Shop Ltd
Whitemill Industrial Estate, Wexford

For Kateřina Wieluchová and
Philip Deane, and in memory
of Bridget O'Sullivan

Contents

I

New Eyes 11
Number Three 12
Old Friends 13
'Iona' Room 14
Circles 15
The House 16
A Winter's Tale 17
Train of Thought 19
Arrival 20
Poem for M 21
Walking into Trinity 22
Birthday 23
Carpe Diem 24
Coming of Age 25
Repetition 26
In a Far Country 27
A Piece of Cake 29
Exotica 30
Painting by Sarah Rushton 31
Sacred Space 32
The Island 33

II

Unholy Ground 37
The Navigator, Cobh 38
On the Move 39
Old Cork 40
Day-Dreaming 41
Romanian in Grand Parade 42
In the Mardyke 43
Psalm 44
Directions 45
The Yellow Rose Café 46

Choirs of Angels   47
Sister Bernadette   48
Horse Show   49
Memories   50
When Woody Died   51
Meditation   52
Starting-Point   53
Eating Out   54
Chapel Girl   55
Moods   56
Forgotten   57
Sonnet   58
The Veil   59

III

Lady of Ceylon   63
El Camino   64
Snowfall   65
Piazza del Commune, Assisi   66
Within   67
Wadding Cloister   68
Getting to Perugia   69
Insomnia   70
Temptation   71
Stop the Car   72
Fioretti   73
The Other Half   74
Personne   75
Treasure Trove   76
  1 Promise Me   76
  2 Meeting   76
  3 Going East   77
  4 Don't Forget   78
  5 Photograph   78
Aubade   80
Trois Couleurs   81

I

Though we travel the world over to find the beautiful, we must carry it with us or we find it not

R. W. EMERSON

New Eyes

Tonight I seem to see you with new eyes,
First mountains, alps of *auld lang syne*.
'Do you recall the once,' my brother said,
'We camped out under Seefin in the cool of June?'

How smooth the car seems on the cambered road.
We miss them first soon after Lemybrien
But here they are again coming to Kilmeaden.
I feel more than a twinge at leaving them behind.

And to think they were faithfully there for me
All those years, all that time I never even gave
Them a thought: Monavullaghs, Crotty's Lake of
Comeragh. Is it pure nostalgia or a thwarted love

For what abides, despite the lure of strange sights
Far away? Age wears away the sandstone of surprise.
Oh, my first mountains, alps of *auld lang syne*,
Tonight I seem to see you with new eyes.

Number Three

When was the last time I went in
The door of that house whose range,
Whose oven, kept us late for school?

The turf was spongy, Hitler had put
Paid to coal; the barrel of sawdust
Stood bone idle in the yard.

To answer my own question, 'more than
Twenty years ago.' Now, two occupants
Later, I mount the mossy steps, insert

A brand new key in the lock, wonder
What I will remember; what's facile
To forget or unbearably hard.

I feel I left in winter with your
Faucets frozen stiff, your larder bare,
Your windows bleared with rain.

Rebuke, rebuke me, once the one and only
World I knew. Like some perplexed lover
You had let me go; I am back again.

Old Friends

It's a homely house and no mistake,
Has been expanded to make
Space for love and room for
Strangers; must have a history
I cannot even hint at.

The longer I visit the more I
Am drawn to the rivers, just sitting
Watching them from the big window;
Sipping tea, munching toast,
Feeling unbelievably contented.

Kealnagower and Finnihy streams,
I awaken after a night of
Non-stop rain to find you almost
Back to your old selves:
Rumbustious, eager to embrace.

Now man-made light shines out from
The glass to leave its starry
Glimmer on your waters. I find the whole
Thing enchanting – you two meeting like
Old friends beyond the bare clematis.

'Iona' Room

There are no doors anywhere
In this room of books and clothes,

Except the door that shuts them all in,
Keeps them tight about the outsize bed:

Clothes that may have seen better days
But are not discarded, just in case

They revive a memory of how something
Occurred that was extra-special;

Volumes that are crying out to be taken
Up and browsed through, if only to say

You have not forgotten how they came to
Sit where they are, came to be yours.

Circles

He never said goodbye; he stole
Away one morning when the sun was
Scarcely up; he said he hated partings.

In us he left behind a need, unspoken
And misunderstood: the day brightened but
The heart did not; it was numb with dread.

In what had been his room for all
Those years we found the remains of a
Take-away; a bluebottle that went round
And round and round, seeking a way out.

The House

Some may wonder why
He bothers but still he
Will persist in returning;
And he stands there, shyly,
In out of the way, hoping against
Hope he won't be noticed.

Not that he has any idea who
Lives there now, but the
Meagre flowers look so poor
In the moonlight. He is abreast
Of little, only there
To contemplate what happened.

When the time came he had
Pulled out the door behind
Him, tightening his grip on
The future, deliberately
Forgetting to look back.

A Winter's Tale

When we were about old enough not to wonder
    any more,
Who should arrive at our door the week before
    Christmas
But the local parish priest, wondering
Would we ever 'do the crib?'

Next day we released them from the back
    sacristy –
The baby in the manger,
Joseph, Mary and a quartet of shepherds.
We dusted down the three Wise Kings –
They were covered in cobwebs.

One was as black as the ace of spades.

We later discovered the cow and the donkey,
The main frame and a Bethlehem backdrop,
That could have done with a lick of paint.
Not that it mattered – the work could begin.

The following day it was off to the wood
For fern and moss, holly and ivy;
And to Tierney's farm for a hammer and crosscut,
Thatch for the roof,
Straw for the stable.

On Christmas morning came the finishing
 touches.
Seldom if ever have we felt so elated.
We threw the switch that lit up the backdrop,
Gazed in awe at our creation.
Would it fall flat on its face or cause a
 sensation?

Train of Thought

He dreamt he was
Walking in Portarlington,
On his arm a
Lady of the Huguenots.

He could smell the scent of
Honeysuckle, the woodbine of
A summer long since gone.

Queen's County was an idea in
Someone's head. Sunday bells
Called the suited and
Bonneted to worship.

A haze of promise hung over
Town and country. South, East and
West would meet at the railway.

Arrival

I've often wanted to be outside myself,
Outside the carriage, and watch it
Coming down the long incline into
The anything but welcoming station.

Oh for someone to be there to assault
Me with a smile I never saw coming,
A hug threatening my surprised vertebrae.

But all my astral body would observe
Must bore it to tears in the extreme.
We loiter reluctantly around trains
And life's for getting on with.

Poem for M

At 'Lillouet' you liked to
Potter round the farmyard,
Handling ancient ploughs and harrows,
Mounting an obsolete reaper-and-binder,
Photographing everything that didn't move.

What a difference a year makes.
You took to pandering to the palate
In the minikin kitchen of 'Clos Neuf.'
I caught you talking to yourself
While playing mother, mixing
Some concoction for baking.

Towards the end of the millennium
Twice you sailed for Brittany.
When I forget to remember I'll still
Remember the apple tree there
Under which you smiled,
The unspoken way you told me,
'Grow up and be your age.'

Walking into Trinity

When you walk in to Trinity
You go the way I went before you
Forty odd years ago,

By Harcourt Street and the Green,
Down Grafton Street, then through
Those not always welcoming gates.

There I often went to watch the
Athletes show their paces on
June grass as green as Ireland.

There you go now to surf the net,
To polish up your French
And make me green with envy.

Forty years! Were I half that time
Again, I would be your confident
Age, saying farewell forever to

The teens, expecting wonders:
Not fearing the future in any shape
Or form, every day a birthday.

Birthday

The years whizz by like trains passing out
Each other. We too have been shunting in
Opposite directions. Why? Don't ask me: I
Might not want to waste my breath explaining.

Linger only long enough to read this just
The once. I can picture you saying, 'Fair enough,
I'll do just that.' But now you've done it
You'll be blowed if you can understand one word.

Thus you have me grabbling somewhere deep in my
Being, hoping that my heart is saying what language
Never could, not even, 'Here's a handsel on
The threshold of your twentieth year: step
In to find surprise surprising you.'

Carpe Diem

The early twenties is a special time:
The start of summer, the tail-end of spring.
I can't quite remember if and when they ever really
    were together
So much did the motto 'Carpe diem' seem the thing.

'Seize the day.' I recall getting up one morning
And there stood a different season at the door.
My ship had sailed, my life had left its harbour;
Happy abandonment, that stage was past, and for sure.

Surely now is a very special time for you: for me
The birth of winter, not quite the death of fall.
Seize the day, I say, both to myself and you: sally
Forth on the high and low tide of spring becoming summer,
    autumn becoming winter: give it your all.

Coming of Age
Time for Sunsets

Are you still too young, I wonder, to make time
For sunsets? I conjure up five cool men, five brothers,
Testing the pristine Ventry sand – in hindsight, the welcome calm
Before the storm of a Kerry wedding weathers

Very nicely. Of course it was morning and we are morning
People; youth alone will still make you so. We even thought
Of dancing before the music started. April was turning
Out right in the end; what we saw was what we actually got.

That day you were only an idea, a notion in the head.
Now time coaxes you daintily towards the way it was
When we broke from that beach; each granule, shingle, seaweed
Wished us well. I thought, make time for sunsets; pause
So that you may savour this moment when you've bid Godspeed
To the upshot of love itself and – don't seek for any cause.

Repetition

'You're off to pastures new,' I said
And having said it, knew she hadn't understood.
She was looking at me as though I had two heads,
Pitying me for trying to predict the future.

'You know things I don't know,' I said,
This time to myself. 'Tomorrow's a bag of tricks:
Don't open it until tomorrow comes, then be prepared
To be surprised by not being surprised.'

Later on that morning I thought of how, when
My father died, I had rummaged through his
Scant papers, come across the results of my
First real exam, penned in his exquisite copperplate.

Every day of this new millennium I feel I am becoming
More like him; and I feel proud that he felt proud
Of the achievement I left behind when, at the
Last century's core, I took off for pastures new.

In a Far Country

On your first visit to the wedding chapel
Balloon a prayer for them up into
The Antigua and Barbudan air:
Then, hopefully, our prayers will meet
Somewhere over the western Atlantic Ocean.

Lord, watch over this couple,
Bless this young man and maiden
Who have journeyed far
To ratify their love.

My thoughts travel to you
In a very frail craft
And, like Brendan and his companions of old,
Will first go by the Hebrides and Orkney,
The Faeroes, Iceland and Greenland:
Then head southwards
To avoid the heart's icebergs.

Lord, watch over this couple,
Bless this young man and maiden
Who have journeyed far
To ratify their love.

There on the shore this morning
He sensed, coming on the breeze
As though from heaven,
The sound of every song he ever knew
Or ever treasured:

He heard, as though sung by an angel,
'The Boys of Wexford.'

Lord, watch over this couple,
Bless this young man and maiden
Who have journeyed far
To ratify their love.

A Piece of Cake

Thanks for sending me that piece of wedding cake
Which had a kick in it like Banjo Patterson's banjo.
When I sampled it I could picture the Gladesville shindig –
Women in floppy hats, sherry, beer and promises.

And your elated father attempting 'The Streets of Abbeyside'
At Henley Bowling, a full octave clean beyond his range,
Stretching his throat out into the bright Sydney afternoon
And nobody, and I mean nobody, finding it all that strange.

Did you come back to late winter as I suspect you did,
Gazing out at Beara coping with its usual quota of rain?
Still, when the last crumb is eaten and the weather clears,
Recall your trip, your raggle-taggle time in Kogarah Bay.

Exotica

From the New World bring me back
A petal from a blossom
On a tree in Central Park.

Stroll in some day when you have
Time and, when no one is looking,
Snatch it from the bough.

But choose its colour carefully:
Remember I don't want anything
That smacks too much of home.

One will do. I don't need New York:
I wish only to have something
Of its future to hold on to.

Occasionally I hope to take it out
And repeat to myself: that's all
I really ever needed of America.

Painting by Sarah Rushton

They surprise me, these yellow poppies.

I can imagine them in the artist's garden,
Bringing joy, being her inspiration.

Here they appear to us on mere cardboard,
Alive no longer but no less tactile.

Growing wild again they would revert surely
To the aura of Flanders, mute erubescence.

Over the years shedding their brightness,
Reminding us then of lipstick sunsets;
The dead recalled, the living remembering.

Sacred Space

In memory of Breda Devon Costello

You were to all a free-born spirit,
A sapling at once fragile and strong:
Gentle too – the gentle the earth shall inherit.
August waned, September came along
And there you were touching my life
With bright ideas about God in us and us in God,

Tantalizing thoughts beckoning us to strive
To be free of the trappings, the onus of the load.

All our suffering comes from desiring things
That cannot be had: stop desiring and you won't get hurt.
That's what Jalal al-Din Rumi wrote and what brings
Release now as I read again your letter.

                                           For all I'm worth
I'll quote from that Sufi sage of your final testament.
Living life to the full is outside morality, not outside prayer:
'Way beyond ideas of right-doing and wrong-doing, of our intent,
There is a field: I, the One, will come to meet you there.'

The Island

We thought we heard the hills talking to each other
That autumn morning as we came ashore.
Out the window went any notion of the misty past, the bother
Caused: we felt a spell we'd never known before.

The heights weren't quite affirming our arrival,
Now russet, now azure, in their displays of light.
Red for vengeance and blood, blue patently frugal
Made any loss of purpose seem an oversight.

Summits were speaking as though we weren't there
At once caressingly, then in a blind rage
As if to set the proverbial heather on fire,
Banish inhabitants, abolish foliage.

Do they sense, I wonder, this confection of hatred and love
By sentinels that go through every mood:
Those glensmen, valley folk, what have they still to prove
And would they want to, even if they could?

II

A new love, a new
litany of place names;
the hill city of Cork ...

JOHN MONTAGUE

Unholy Ground

We cut the engine and the whale appeared,
All alone now in the vast harbour, deep
Enough for the tears of a million partings.

The four seasons in one afternoon. Arriving
In rain, cruising in Arctic air: later watching
Water and sky alter from spring to summer.

Bowing in prayer at the Cathedral, how many,
I wonder, had time or energy to climb up here
Before setting off to Philadelphia in the morning?

My thoughts speed out to Roche's Point, then
Wheel westwards in the frail boat of memory.
Painfully we learn the lessons of history, that
The whale must die or return to the open sea.

The Navigator, Cobh

A little paper boat,
   Only it isn't paper;
A pet summer's day,
   Only it isn't summer.
The boat is cupped in
   The Navigator's hands.

His pointed nose
   Points towards the harbour;
His lower torso's embedded
   In a ship's prow.
Just looking at him
   Is making me seasick.

A little paper boat,
   Only it isn't paper;
It's cast-iron, as are
   The Navigator's torso,
His biceps, his face
   With the peaky nose.

I hope to dream tonight
   The cast-iron turns to paper;
That the little paper boat
   Leaves its paper nest,
Rises with the moon
   To sail on a paper ocean.

On the Move

This morning I heard
A cello moaning in
Patrick's Street, lamenting
My arrival in Cork.
I escaped into Carey's
Lane, then offered a hasty
Prayer in Saint Peter & Paul's,
Smelt the incense of exile.

Old Cork

Here is a place
Well equipped for the rains,
Flooding inevitable
When the waters rise.

In Grand Parade
Ghosts rear their inquisitive heads,
Prise open the patience
Of shopper and shopkeeper.

You smell coffee, chocolate,
Hear a strange amalgam of accents,
Though all from the same tone poem.

Talking's being set to music,
Conversation is serious business,
To be teased out and savoured.

This is a proud city:
And when the bells chime out
And make the tourist stop and think
There might be a God after all

And, in the next breath,
Wonder what all the fuss is about,
I realise I, too, am a stranger here,
Will be always a stranger.

Day-Dreaming

My gaze looks north towards
Gurranabraher. Shades of Kavanagh,
His black hills, Gortin, Shancoduff.

From my window I can glance down
At the dead fountain, the red roses
Still there in bloom as winter comes.

Roofs have lost their gloss with
The years' passage, not so the flowers.
They will fade only on the table.

Nothing's better than just standing here
A November morning, watching the yawning
Light playing on the weathered tiles,

Day-dreaming of the way Cork used to look
Much more like Granada, housetops blood-red
Like the roses, below them the river in spate.

Romanian in Grand Parade

As I came around 'The Roundy'
There she was, gathering courage
To ask for my loose change,

But she hadn't the language yet
To explain herself properly and
I was laden down with baggage.

She uttered never a word, and what
Could have trumped that? The silence
Was deafening, it said everything.

Half-hearted light stole over
The laid-back piazza. I, as indifferent
As the pigeons, went home crushed.

In the Mardyke

Where the river, now my river, was in
Overflow, I came on women, two women,
Twittering like birds on wires.

One introduced me to the other – she
Who had read widely and so deeply loved
A man who was the apple of her eye.

How I wished I had read and loved like that:
Then we might not have twittered, chattered on
About cats and dogs and things; we might have

Shared our dreams that seem not to make sense.
Flow on, swift river, through this loquacious day,
Get thee to places we can never reach.

Psalm

It was indeed a golden time:
My heart sang all day long.
I was roused by morning's benediction
With its hope and ample light.
Night took me, like a tired child,
Under its colourful duvet of sleep.

Still I dream of an episode that
Will never come again, even now
Improbable in the scheme of things.
Time tinkers with accurate memory.
Was it truly so or do I deceive
Myself as never before or since?

I awake to the sound of dawn in a
Strange city. Love has bivouacked
Here a thousand years, absorbed again
And again and again a quiet symphony
Of peace. I await only the last
Caterwaul. As it was, is and will be.

Directions

A town split by the road from
The metropolis to the west;
A town scarcely a town at all.
Here this August day I must
Be looking woebegone,
Awaiting a bus to take me
I don't know where.

Intimate shops, a bank
Not opening every day,
The Main Street missing the
Hustle and bustle of school.
The little river flowing
Through almost unnoticed,
The churchyard roses
Feeling lonesome too.

The whole place
Getting the stranger down –
Not being geared for strangers,
Only for those who live there,
Or leave only to return to the
Embrace of weekends, sometimes
Never to depart again.

A town with a mind of its own,
A town that never comes alive,
Yet seldom seems to sleep.
Here I ease my bag into the
Sarcophagus of the long
Overdue Galway bus. Yes, says
The driver, we are heading east.

The Yellow Rose Café

It was only some place
That I saw from the bus,
Noticed because I was looking out
   the window
Streaked with summer rain, one more
Time listening to Tchaikovsky.
Allegro con fuoco,
The end of that concerto,
Outside the Yellow Rose Café
In Rochfortbridge.

My heart was in my boots,
My arms were windmills;
In my dreams I was drifting,
It was snowing in Siberia;
I was sawing the air in time to
   the piano.
Allegro con fuoco,
The end of that concerto,
Outside the Yellow Rose Café
In Rochfortbridge.

How I wished it were Moate,
Tyrellspass or Kilbeggan;
How I wanted Mozart, Haydn, Brahms, why
   even Beethoven
And the red roses of June but no,
No, no, it just had to be Tchaikovsky.
Allegro con fuoco,
The end of that concerto,
Outside the Yellow Rose Café
In Rochfortbridge.

Choirs of Angels
For Sr. Mary Walsh

When I heard the children singing
I didn't think you taught them songs
But rather how to sing,
Which is quite a different thing.

It's the difference
Between occupation and vocation,
Between sowing and reaping;
Arrival, not departure.

How to find one's soul and
Then, having found it,
Reveal it unashamedly
To the world.

So that it can be said
Without a shade of doubt:
It's not just singing
But a future on the line,
A life in flight –
The singer lost in song.

Sister Bernadette

Nevers for nougatine candies
And fine porcelain, but what I
Remember most is the nook at
St-Gildard, picturing you there
Amid the lilies and roses.

You were to end your days
In peaceful urban Burgundy,
Your peasant hands shaping
Marvels, cherishing the sick
As though Christ come back.

But seldom could you forget
The dizzy past: like when you
Recalled the Lady revealing
Who she was, you would revert
To the patois of home.

Horse Show

Sister Mary Patrice,
Take it easy with the bells,
Be gentle as a dove.
The message is – they
Are worrying the horses,
Which may shy at anything,
Like sensitive contemplatives.

What is prayer to your ears
In your cut-stone enclosure
Spells panic for the thoroughbreds,
The ponies and stallions,
Not to speak of their owners.

You approach in bare feet
To ring another Angelus:
Spare a thought for your friends
In the jumping arena:
Be as thoughtful as Clare,
As forebearing as Francis.

Memories

Do dogs have memories
Like we do, I wonder.
What is he thinking of, there
On the beach all alone?

Where is his master – or
Is it his mistress?
Where have the crowds gone, those
Children who threw him the bone?

Doggie, Doggie, tell me your
Name and come when I call.
But he is as quiet as death,
By the camera frozen in time.

In the silence, the silence
He patiently watches and waits.
He gazes and gazes into the far
Distant future, and nobody comes.

When Woody Died

When Woody died
You went and sprinkled
Holy water on his grave
In the field beyond the barn.
This dumb inoffensive creature
Was twelve and you fourteen.

Poor theology but perfect
Logic? Not logical at all.
You craved that he might
Live on, albeit in some
Different way, that your wish
Might bring him back.

Last night I dreamt he came again
And, when the house was quiet save
For the ticking of the kitchen clock,
Curled up before the stove;
A little bundle of warmth
Proclaiming its resurrection.

Meditation

No one that's ever been
Relaxes quite like this tabby,
A yogi needing nobody,
Her mind a *tabula rasa*.

True, after siesta, it will fill
Up again with thoughts of food
Or love or both: a lake of milk,
Some hopeful tom coming to call.

But just now she sinks into
Plush on-the-spot cushions.
Above her, I'm the inverse of the
Yeti, visible yet not quite real.

Starting-Point

We got the name from Old English,
Took it from 'Ēostre,' the
Anglo-Saxon goddess of spring.

A most benign and gentle
Influence; bounteous and fruitful;
Generous to a fault.

Maybe which is why I find my Lord,
My Love, arising too in cherry,
Cowslip and daffodil; camellia,
Magnolia, wild hyacinth.

Eating Out
For Patricia

I have ceased cooking professionally,
Creating mouth-watering soda bread
In that immaculate kitchen
For the ravenous Wexford friars.

They say they will miss me but,
Remembering the speed with which
They dispatched my flans and pastas,
Do they mean myself or what I concocted?

Now more than ever I love eating out,
Being waited upon: with a finicky
Knowing smile, picking and choosing
From the *table d'hôte* of life.

Chapel Girl

Bent in supplication, her
Face in her hands, knees and
Shoulders in tandem, her lips
The lips of the dead.

She expects no answer, not because
Nobody is listening but rather
That nothing means anything.

Not anymore. No thought to be had,
No emotion endured, no hope that the
Numbness will melt into joy or tears.

How did I get here, she muses,
And will my heart howl in grief,
The ground support me, once I
Attempt to walk in the sun?

Moods

Sometimes I would become
Alarmed for no reason.
For days the nimbus settled
On every butte and hillock.

And then the dimness lifted.
I would ascend to view the mottled
Bay: so many coloured islands
On the milky crust of ocean.

Don't even attempt to comprehend
What's going on in my mind: or
Ask am I fey or what; for the
Birds, away with the fairies.

Forgotten

I must have been here
The best part of a year
When one morning, out of the blue,
I took to cleaning my room.

To my utter amazement
The variegated floor
Took on a spit and polish look;
My once burdened desk
Came up amber in the peerless light.

And there,
In every nook and cranny
Of the only space I can call my own,
Were the unmistakable signs of her presence,
Years and years before, of course.

Devotedly she must have hurried
From wheelchair to bedside and back,
Nursing that now equally forgotten invalid –
In her give-away stiletto heels.

Sonnet

This poem might have been obvious many moons ago
But not before what happened happened.
She was to skip the part about the lost portfolio,
Home in instead on what drove her round the bend.
It was the way he talked only about himself,
How, day in day out, he was strapped for cash;
Got by on scraps dished up on cardboard delph
Or, what he could ill afford, bangers and mash.
It was as though he could fill canvas after canvas,
Dawns and gloamings lived out under the stars,
While she remembered saws like 'Live horse and eat grass'
Or songs, 'I've got you under my skin,' the first few bars.
She was to feel his absence like an afterglow,
The poem she wrote being everything she could know.

The Veil

We sailed for Sherkin
On a turquoise sea.
Blue turned to green,
Then back to blue again.

That same evening the roused
Dead greeted our arrival.

They had risen from their graves
With the minimum of fuss and,
In groups of twos and threes,
Made for the pier.

Had they thought to surprise us
They were set to fail.
Death and life are part of
The one partitioned room.
The girl-next-door who
Died is but a veil away.

I thought I recognised the
Odd face here and there.

What caught my eye was
The pallor of their visage,
The sameness of manner and
Bearing and, look till the
Cows come home, you could
Not distinguish man from
Woman, boy from child.

Nothing was said, either
By them or us but we
Never set foot on the
Island and that's a fact.

They saw us off in silence, then
Returned to where they came from.
Once clear of the harbour wall, a
Great peace descended on our boat.

III

Ho ripassato
le epoche
della mia vita

Questi sono
i miei fiumi

GIUSEPPE UNGARETTI

Lady of Ceylon

From her I learned the ritual of making tea.
Even the way she said 'a cup of tea' sent a
Pulse, a ripple of expectation through me.

As she dunked two spoonfuls of sugar in my cup
I thought of one as Tamil, one Sinhalese,
Sweetening Sri Lanka, bitter tear dropped

From Asia into the Indian Ocean. As I recall,
My heart melted like sugar in the hot tea
She loved to stir for me. With what infinite

Concern she added the milk – to that miracle
Degree of coolness, my lips would neither
Be scalded nor lose their own sure fire.

El Camino

I rub my flesh on stone in
Santiago, that well-worn granite
Caressed by artist and musician,
Beggar and thief, pauper and peasant,
Saint and king, virgin and whore.

Here may my stiff body and more
Stubborn heart be taught the secret
Of the inner journey, the one not yet
Begun but, once begun, will
Never end, or end outside of time.

One night in the Picos de Europa
I found myself dreaming in Castilian,
A strange dream awash with poetry
And omens. Dawn came unmercifully
Early: we pressed towards Astorga.

I will return in another year, make
Of this pilgrimage a lighter step.
Meantime I soar to the high altar,
Press my fingers into the 'Root of
Jesse,' then clutch my 'compostella.'

Snowfall

For Raphael Huang Chi-Tsai

Even after a couple of months
Of trying to learn English
You still didn't know what poetry meant,
The word I mean.

If and when you spoke at all
It was to answer questions
Monosyllabically –
Cup, plate, knife, fork, yes, no.

But then came the day you were to experience
Snow for the first time.
It closed the airport and
You missed your connection home to Taiwan.

All of which meant that, on the
Morning after the Feast of the Holy Innocents,
You could visit the enclosed Poor Clares.

We are told that your long-suffering tongue
Was loosened in such company.

They listened as only they can; you spoke
As never before. You were
Poetry in motion,
Chinese music to their ears.

Piazza del Commune, Assisi

Do you remember this place,
Where nobody clock-watches,
Tourists are nursing coffees,
Locals mention the earthquakes?

To here we gravitate when the
Sun gets to our best intentions.
We suck from the fountain,
The sweat of an Umbrian noon
Still wet on our cheeks.

And night-time is best here,
Night-time is 'other-world.'
On the Calends of May
Young students from Pisa and Lucca
Dance out of their skins.

Within

Don't be deceived by the
Rather posh black and gold scaffolding
On the street-side of tall houses.
Within may be chaos.

The blonde waitress at Pozzo Romana
Laughed when she broke a tumbler on the floor
But her mind wasn't with us.

She was recalling that evening
A cupboard opened before her very eyes;
All its delph and cutlery
Poured out onto her lap.

When the lights came on again
There was shattered glass everywhere,
Tufts of dust in her hair.

I feel rather sorry for these people
Who have abandoned their homes, perhaps forever,
To live on sympathy, comfortless crumbs.

Wadding Cloister

Here surely grow
    The world's worst oranges;
Rosalba harvests them
    To make robust marmalade.

Passing by the laundry
    Each afternoon before siesta,
I praise her cooking,
    We exchange pleasantries.

Her iron aloft in a
    Plethora of gestures,
She smiles out at me
    From aprons and dishcloths.

Getting to Perugia

Getting to Perugia was like
Attempting to get into heaven
And every bit as difficult.

We missed buses and trains;
It took all of three hours
To crawl twenty miles.

We were as children in the
Limbo of Italian timetables. Ponte
San Giovanni was purgatory.

At Sant'Anna we soared on the
Escalators, then stepped out
Into wind and punishing rain.

If only we knew it, in fickle
Perugia we had lost our
Chance to experience Paradise.

Insomnia

Homesick without quite knowing it, I drifted back
To the car, escorted by soft-bodied fireflies,
Phosphorescent sparklers dilating the late summer air.
Then, as most nights, the moon was a camembert.

Its light pervaded the room, shone through the latticed
Windows, denying me sleep. Laser pinpricks played
On the white ceiling. I was in two places at once,
If you know what I mean. In Umbria I felt Breton.

Later, at Point du Raz, I would gaze down into the savage
Finistère sea, recall the cheese-shaped moon and what it
Did for me; those flies that tantalizingly danced above
The quiet cobbled streets of that city renowned for peace.

Temptation

Life in Anjou, you know,
Isn't all roses and wine.

After several rainy days I
Finally succumb to temptation,
Go price umbrellas in the
Covered market of Cholet.

The young girl seizes her
Opportunity, comes as near as
She can to lamenting the weather.

What was it my father used say, quoting
The old song? 'Let your smile be your
Umbrella, even on a rainy day.'

Stop the Car

We only drove over the brow of a hillock
And there we were, viewing the landscape
Of the paintings. I have experienced the million
Rainbows of Chartres, seen Paris at night
From the air and survived, and now this.

I wish I could explain it but it is as
It was – canvas uneasy on easel, poised
Unguent brush asking no quarter. One day come
And see it for yourselves; and stop the car,
Look as far as the eye can see, daydream
A thousand art galleries in an instant.

Recall, don't ever forget, what came
First. The sinewy cathedral of poplars,
Wheat golden twice over in the evening sun,
Farmsteads seemingly forsaken and the colours,
The colours – their combination – there just then
On the wet line of life hung out to dry.

Fioretti

How difficult it proved that day
To leave Le Loroux-Bottereau.

Somewhere out in the suburbs
There were signs pointing everywhere,
Roads leading to all our tomorrows
But we hadn't found them.

Vallet and Clisson beckoned
As did Champtoceaux to the north.

More in desperation than anything else
We remembered Francesco Bernardone.

You spun our compliant car
Round and round at the crossroads:
It stopped facing Beaupréau.

The Other Half

That evening at Solesmes
    Wasn't all gloom.
Half a hundred monks
    Chanted office as though
Their very lives depended on it;
    The other half had come
To listen, maybe learn
    Something, go with the flow.

More than likely learn one
    Is better off not knowing
The future – what's coming,
    What's around the bend.
For instance, the road to Laval
    Never asked where we were going:
Make no mistake, we were
    To get there in the end.

Ever since, when I recall
    Those voices in the choir,
I think of souls set free
    To fly out of their pain
Into the mystical regions of
    Surprise, reaching to where
We sense tomorrow's promise
    After days of rain.

Personne

Madonna, you are special because you
Have no name and no cult and I ought
To have left you where I found you,
Anonymous amidst the beads and holy icons.

But I bought you for four hundred francs.
I hold you between my palms when I pray,
Trusting you are not too lonely for Solesmes.

Your hands are saying everything, like
'Believe me, I won't reveal your secrets.'
One minute you are accepting, receiving;
The next giving all there is to give.

Madonna, you are heavy, worth your weight
In stone, all simplicities rolled into one.
The monks blessed you before you left them,
Now you are the new woman in my life.

Treasure Trove

1   *Promise Me*

Promise me you won't complain
Too much about the Irish weather
Because when I finish my labour of love
And all your birthdays arrive together

In one treasure trove,
You won't know what hit you then.
Your heart will be light as a feather,
You will even laugh at the rain.

We are only passing through, you and I,
With just so much to discover;
Our minds open to explore
Pathways that cannot but sever.

Leaving the familiar shore
With no star to travel by,
Sometimes saying 'never say never,'
Sometimes 'never say goodbye.'

2   *Meeting*

Don't expect bulk around my shoulders
Or difference lower down. Should I come
Threadbare into your stomping-ground
Don't feel one bit surprised.

Ideas speed like arrows to the nub
Of the talk. There they abide
Now, sibilant and comfortable,
In feathers that cannot embarrass.

Irony lingers playfully at the edge
Of each insight. I come as I am,
Take me or leave me; then you appear.
We meet as though words in a poem.

3 Going East

Děstník, yes; even your
Umbrella becomes you:
It hints at a seriousness
I can adjust to.

I behold your city
Ringing in my heart,
A woman become a song
Woven into time.

It is getting closer
To when we walk – under
Your umbrella, of course –
The streets of Seifert's Prague.

Open it, even if it isn't
Raining, and we will go together
To the Old Jewish Cemetery
And rain our tears.

4 Don't Forget

I'm afraid to kiss your cheeks
In case the skin should crack:
I'm almost afraid to say you're
  beautiful
Just in case you didn't know.

What makes you real is the
Way you can coax your hair
To hide inside your coat
From collar to waist
And manage it without
Worrying where it's gone.

Once you shot away on your
Second-hand yellow bicycle.
Some day you won't come back –
Daughter I never had.

But first remember to remind
Me: don't forget the roses.

5 Photograph

The way you're sitting at the table
Who would ever dream you're homesick
Though I caught you several times yesterday
Already yearning for tomorrow.

Not in so many words, more in the way
You signal with those dark eyes. Somehow
The evening light dims a little: I
Have a presentiment of pain.

Then as we part you hunch up, you walk
Away with something of a hangdog look.
I feel guilty at your sadness, that I can't
Spirit you back there and then to home.

Aubade

Sing the song of parting
Which I saw in your face
As you sipped your coffee.

Sense the pulse of things,
The first leaves falling,
The wood agog with expectation.

And, as the paper cup emptied,
So empty your heart for autumn
Arriving like a thief in the night.

Trois Couleurs

After Krzysztof Kieślowski

My eyes were red when we parted:
I held your hands for a moment;
They were blue with the cold.

Afterwards I watched the snow falling.
Now my days will be silent as the grave.

Until the first notes of spring sound
In the forest, I will lament your going,
The waning of the white heat of desire.